W9-ATT-697

BEYONCÉ
QUEEN OF THE SPOTLIGHT

>>TRAIL BLAZERS

Neil Armstrong

Jackie Robinson

Harriet Tubman

Jane Goodall

Albert Einstein

Beyoncé

>>TRAIL BLAZERS

BEYONCÉ
QUEEN OF THE SPOTLIGHT

**EBONY JOY
WILKINS**

RANDOM HOUSE  NEW YORK

Text copyright © 2020 by Ebony Joy Wilkins
Cover art copyright © 2020 by Luisa Uribe and George Ermos
Interior illustrations copyright © 2020 by Artful Doodlers
Trailblazers logo design by Mike Burroughs
Additional images used under license from Shutterstock.com

All rights reserved. Published in the United States by Random House Children's Books,
a division of Penguin Random House LLC, New York.

Random House and the colophon are registered trademarks of Penguin Random House LLC.

Visit us on the Web! rhcbooks.com

Educators and librarians, for a variety of teaching tools, visit us at
RHTeachersLibrarians.com

Library of Congress Cataloging-in-Publication Data
Name: Wilkins, Ebony, author.
Title: Beyoncé : Queen of the spotlight / Ebony Joy Wilkins.
Description: New York: Random House Children's Books, 2020. | Series: Trailblazers |
Includes bibliographical references and index.
Identifiers: LCCN 2019031507 | ISBN 978-0-593-12443-7 (trade pbk.) |
ISBN 978-0-593-12444-4 (lib. bdg.) | ISBN 978-0-593-12445-1 (ebook)
Subjects: LCSH: Beyoncé, 1981– —Juvenile literature. |
Singers—United States—Biography—Juvenile literature.
Classification: LCC ML3930.K66 W55 2020 | DDC 782.42164092 [B]—dc23

Created by Stripes Publishing Limited, an imprint of the Little Tiger Group

Printed in the United States of America
10 9 8 7 6 5 4 3 2 1

First Edition

Contents

REACHING FOR THE STARS

On January 31, 2010, at the Fifty-Second Annual Grammy Awards, a young woman owned the stage at the Staples Center in Los Angeles. She was already so famous that she was known all over the world by just one name: Beyoncé.

That evening, in front of a live audience of almost 20,000 music professionals and influencers, as well as over 25 million television viewers, Beyoncé won award after award and brought the whole audience to its feet with stunning performances of two songs. No one could have doubted that the girl from Houston, Texas, was doing what she was born to do.

⋛ A SPECIAL NIGHT ⋚

This wasn't the first time the superstar had stepped onstage to accept a Grammy. In fact, during her relatively short career, she'd already won ten of the special awards. But on this particular night, Beyoncé had been nominated for ten Grammys, more than anyone else present, and would take home six—in 2010, that was the most awards that any female artist had ever won in one night.

Beyoncé's Big Wins

→ Song of the Year for "Single Ladies (Put a Ring on It)"

→ Best Female Pop Vocal Performance for "Halo"

→ Best Female R&B Vocal Performance for "Single Ladies (Put a Ring on It)"

→ Best Traditional R&B Vocal Performance for "At Last"

→ Best R&B Song for "Single Ladies (Put a Ring on It)"

→ Best Contemporary R&B Album for *I Am . . . Sasha Fierce*

The Grammys

The Grammys are music's equivalent
of the Oscars for movies.
The annual ceremony features
performances by famous artists
and the presentation of the main
awards. Nominations for awards are
made by music industry professionals—it is
an honor to be nominated and to be asked to
perform. Beyoncé is the most nominated woman
in the history of the Grammys.

The golden Grammy trophies are in the
shape of old-fashioned gramophones, early
machines on which music could be played.
In fact, the awards are engraved after the
ceremony, so on the night of the ceremony,
winners are given "stunt" awards as stand-
ins for the real thing.

As the announcers read the name of the song
"Halo" on the winner's card, the crowd roared in
celebration. Dressed in a dazzling silver gown,
Beyoncé climbed the stairs toward the stage.

She hugged her Grammy close to her chest and took a deep breath. "I'm sorry, I'm nervous," she said, addressing the audience. "This has been such an amazing night for me and I'd love to thank the Grammys. I'd love to thank my family for all of their support, including my husband. I love you."

MATHEW KNOWLES

For Beyoncé, music is not just a career. It's the way she expresses herself. It's family—literally. The singer's father, Mathew, was her manager for many years. Her mother, Tina, made costumes and styled her. Her sister, Solange, performed as a backup dancer during several of her shows, and has also become an award-winning singer herself. Beyoncé's husband, the rapper, songwriter, and producer Jay-Z, has worked and toured with her while pursuing his own very successful career.

TINA KNOWLES

SOLANGE KNOWLES

JAY-Z

That night in 2010 would have been a high point in anyone's career, but Beyoncé has never been one to stand still. All her life, she has pushed herself to do better, stretching herself and developing her talents in exciting ways. That evening in Los Angeles was no exception. Even as she accepted the awards and applause of her peers, Beyoncé had plans to take her life in a new direction.

Refusing to be trapped by her success and fame, she took a break from performing for several months and decided to no longer be managed by her father. Her growth as an artist, far from having reached its peak, was only just beginning.

> I don't have to prove anything to anyone. I only have to follow my heart and concentrate on what I want to say to the world. I run my world.

⋛ INSPIRATIONS ⋚

Although many people see Beyoncé as a fresh and electrifying force among music artists, she has always been inspired by those who have gone before. A trip to a Michael Jackson concert when she was a child was an early influence. Later, she admired and absorbed the artistry of legends such as Diana Ross and Prince. Her own success led to her working professionally with many of those who had fueled her dreams as a young girl.

Diana Ross

Diana Ross was born on March 26, 1944, in Detroit, Michigan. As a teenager, Ross was the lead singer of Motown's legendary group the Supremes. The group performed all around the world and sang the hit songs "Where Did Our Love Go"  and "Stop! In the Name of Love." After she left the Supremes, Ross went on to release several solo albums, the first of which featured the anthem "Ain't No Mountain High Enough."

In the 2006 movie *Dreamgirls*, a fictional account of a girl group similar to the Supremes, Beyoncé played the part of Deena Jones, a role based on Diana Ross's career. On March 26, 2019, Beyoncé joined Ross's family and friends to serenade 75-year-old Diana at her birthday party at the Hollywood Palladium.

Prince

On June 7, 1958, Prince Rogers Nelson was born in Minneapolis, Minnesota. Prince grew up in a musical home. His parents were jazz musicians and performed in the Prince Rogers Band. As a child, Prince listened to his parents and discovered his own love of music. He taught himself to play the piano, guitar, and drums and to write songs—he hoped to join his parents onstage someday.

His talent as a singer, songwriter, and music producer inspired many artists, including Beyoncé. His R&B and pop albums reached the top of the *Billboard* charts, and he won seven Grammys. His highest-selling album, *Purple Rain*, sold 1.5 million copies in the first week. On February 8, 2004, Beyoncé joined her idol onstage for a five-minute set at the 46th Grammy Awards to perform a medley of his songs. He died on April 21, 2016, at Paisley Park, his home in Minnesota.

$\gtrless$ THE PATH TO STARDOM $\gtrless$

Beyoncé was born to perform. At the age of five, she was already singing and dancing across her living room for anyone who would watch. She copied her favorite artists from TV recordings, practicing over and over to perfect her singing and her dance moves. Before long, she was doing the rounds at local talent shows and singing auditions.

At nine, she fronted a girl band called Girls Tyme. It wasn't an easy road for the young performers. The group went through disappointments, and its membership changed, but by the time the group altered its name to Destiny's Child in 1996, its members were well on the way to stardom and winning Grammys of their own.

In 2001, the highly successful Destiny's Child took a break to pursue solo careers. Beyoncé was the last of the three members to release a solo album, but when she did so in 2003, it was a huge success. Somehow she also found time to pursue an acting career.

With her life under constant scrutiny from the press, every move analyzed, Beyoncé manages to present a wholesome and aspirational image for young fans. It's impossible to overestimate the global impact this legendary performer has.

On that night in January 2010, Beyoncé's most successful bestselling albums were yet to come, along with her iconic performances at the Super Bowl and Coachella. But the seeds of her future were already apparent in her fierce and fearless stage performances and the ever-growing numbers of fans who loved her boldness and her beauty as well as her music.

CHAPTER 1

A SUPERSTAR IS BORN

Beyoncé Giselle Knowles was born on September 4, 1981, at Park Plaza Hospital in Houston, Texas. Her name was inspired by her mother's French maiden name, Beyincé, which means "beyond others." When Beyoncé was born, her name was unique, but nowadays there are hundreds of girls named in honor of the original Bey.

Beyoncé's father, Mathew, was originally from Gadsden, Alabama. Born into a poor family at a time when African Americans had fewer opportunities because of racism, he worked hard to become a successful businessman. He sold office and medical equipment for Xerox, moving up through the ranks to achieve an important role in the company by the time Beyoncé arrived. Beyoncé's mother, Célestine "Tina" Knowles, was the youngest of seven children in Galveston, Texas. Also a hard worker, Tina was a qualified beautician, with her own salon called Headliners. Not long after Beyoncé was born, Tina returned to work and left her baby girl in the care of Mathew's mother, Lue Helen. Mathew and Tina were supportive and loving, and together they created a comfortable life for themselves and their daughter.

In 1982, when Beyoncé was four months old, her parents bought a three-bedroom, two-story redbrick home in Riverside Terrace, near Houston's museum district. The house had high ceilings and a spiral staircase and a beautiful garden outdoors.

Houston was an exciting place to grow up. With hundreds of shops and restaurants, along with livestock shows, rodeos, and music festivals, **there was** always something going on in the city.

MUSIC IN THE FAMILY

Both of Beyoncé's parents had entered talent shows while growing up, and Tina had been in a singing group called the Beltones when she was in junior high school. Music filled their home, and Beyoncé loved to hear her parents singing gospel, soul, and R&B songs around the house. The radio was always on, blaring out popular hits, and by the time she was three years old, Beyoncé could sing along to her favorites. She liked Michael Jackson's music the most and entertained herself for hours dancing along to his tracks.

My parents used to sing to me all the time. My dad tells me that as a baby, I would go crazy whenever I heard music, and I tried to dance before I could even walk.

A Musical Moment

In the early 2000s, one of the most popular genres of music was rhythm and blues, known as R&B. The musical movement had originated in the 1940s, when African American artists began playing upbeat bluesy-jazz tunes, with a strong beat and soulful vocals. Some early R&B groups include the Cardinals, the Swallows, and the Clovers.

Over the years, R&B evolved to include soul and funk music. Today, music referred to as R&B sounds very different from the songs of the 1940s. Many R&B performers have been influenced by other genres, including hip-hop and pop, creating the styles of artists including Usher, Alicia Keys, and Jennifer Hudson. The Grammys introduced an award for Best R&B Song in 1969.

THE SWALLOWS

One day, Beyoncé's parents surprised her with life-changing news: she was going to see her idol, Michael Jackson, in concert! The wait was torture, but when the day finally arrived, Tina helped Beyoncé pick a special outfit and get ready.

One of the youngest kids in the stadium, Beyoncé took her seat and waited for Michael to arrive onstage. Finally, the opening act ended, the lights dimmed, and her idol stepped out. When Beyoncé saw the "King of Pop," it triggered a passion for performance that would change her life forever.

"If it wasn't for Michael Jackson, I would never ever have performed. . . ."
—Beyoncé

Michael waved a silver-gloved hand, moonwalked across the stage on his tiptoes, and sang his most popular songs, including "Thriller," "Billie Jean," and "Beat It." Beyoncé mouthed the words along with him and tried to memorize his moves. When she got home, she imitated what she'd seen onstage.

SISTERLY LOVE

When Beyoncé was five, the family moved again. Their new home was in Houston's upscale and predominantly African American neighborhood of Third Ward, one of six historical districts in the southeast part of the large city. Not long after the family settled in, Beyoncé's younger sister, Solange Piaget Knowles, was born on June 24, 1986. Beyoncé liked to help look after her sister, bathing, dressing, and feeding Solange alongside her mother.

As soon as Solange could keep up, the girls began to play together and got into all kinds of mischief, but they didn't argue much. On one occasion, Beyoncé came into her room to find toys scattered across the floor. She knew right away who the culprit was, but when she asked her little sister about the mess, Solange denied it! Beyoncé was annoyed, but she liked having a younger sister to look after, so she didn't stay mad at Solange for long.

The girls had a tight bond and respected each other's differences. Beyoncé was shy and introverted, whereas Solange was outgoing and enjoyed socializing and meeting new people.

⇉ STRUGGLES AT SCHOOL ⇇

Beyoncé attended St. Mary's Elementary, a private
Catholic school with an extensive music program.
Beyoncé was excited to start lessons but hesitant about
joining other students, as she hadn't spent much time
around kids her age. She found it hard to fit in and felt
too shy to raise her hand in class.

> Every morning when
> the teacher would take
> roll call, I wanted to
> crawl under my desk.

Her classmates could be unkind, teasing her about
her unusual name and the fact that she spent so much
time by herself. They also made fun of the way she
looked, calling her "ugly" and "chubby" and laughing
at the shape of her ears. "When I was little, my head
was smaller and I looked like I had big Dumbo ears,"
Beyoncé later said.

Math class was a struggle, and one of her fellow
students said Beyoncé was stupid when she couldn't

work out the answer to an equation. Beyoncé tried to ignore the comments and focus on the positive things about school life, like dance classes and singing in the choir, but the name-calling got to her. Tina and Mathew soon noticed that she wasn't being invited to birthday parties or sleepovers and that she never talked about her friends. They became worried that she had none.

⋝ A FIRST PERFORMANCE ⋜

Despite her shyness, Beyoncé did not go unnoticed. Her teacher Darlette Johnson watched her seven-year-old student practicing alone during dance class. She could see the little girl had real talent. One day after class, Darlette began humming a song while cleaning up the studio. Beyoncé, waiting for her ride home, hummed along, too. When Darlette reached the highest notes in the song, she heard Beyoncé hit each note right on key! Darlette asked her student to sing another tune, and Beyoncé's clear, strong voice filled the room. That was when the teacher realized just how talented Beyoncé was. "She can sing. She can really sing!" Darlette said to Mathew and Tina when they arrived to pick up their daughter.

The school was sponsoring a local talent show, and Darlette thought Beyoncé should enter. Mathew and Tina agreed it was a great idea. It would mostly be teenagers performing, and Beyoncé was only seven, but Darlette and her parents felt the talent show would encourage her to step outside of her shell. The three of them helped Beyoncé prepare, and selected a popular song, "Imagine" by John Lennon. The song is about peace and freedom— emotions Beyoncé clearly felt when she was singing and dancing—so it seemed a perfect fit. She learned the lyrics quickly, along with some simple choreography, a sequence of steps or movements that make up a dance routine.

Backstage at the talent show, Beyoncé sang scales to warm up her voice and paced back and forth to calm her nerves. "She would literally have tears in her eyes," Darlette later said about Beyoncé's early performances. "I would have to hold on to her and tell her, 'It's okay. Take deep breaths.'" Once Beyoncé's name was called, she walked out onto the stage. She chose a spot to stare at on the far wall, above the eager sea of faces, and focused on Lennon's lyrics. The room was oddly quiet. In that moment, no one called her chubby. No one made fun of her ears. Every eye was fixed on the young singer as her beautiful voice filled the room.

She spread her arms wide and belted out the lyrics like an experienced performer. Even her parents were shocked at her stage presence! When Beyoncé held the last note, the audience cheered loudly. Several of her classmates who had previously been unkind gave her a standing ovation.

Her first solo performance had been a total success. Incredibly, she won the whole talent show! Beyoncé was overwhelmed with joy, and Mathew, Tina, and Darlette were extremely proud. They decided to nurture her talent by searching for more opportunities to encourage her dream.

THE TROPHIES ROLL IN

After her talent show win, Beyoncé's parents began to enter her in more competitions around Houston. Over the next few years, she appeared in more than fifty shows, some that included beauty contests. Though Beyoncé was much more interested in singing than in walking the runway, winning in the beauty category helped her become more comfortable with her body image. Tina's mother, Agnèz, had been a dressmaker and had passed her skills on to her daughter. Tina made Beyoncé a colorful, sparkly outfit for each competition. Her shelves were soon full of trophies!

In 1988, Beyoncé's parents entered her in her first national competition, the prestigious Sammy Awards, a talent show held in honor of the entertainer Sammy Davis Jr. She achieved first place in the Baby Junior talent category. In her acceptance speech, Beyoncé thanked her family for their support and blew the audience a kiss, like a seasoned professional. Her performance landed her a mention in the *Houston Chronicle*.

The following year, she returned to the show and wowed the audience with a mature performance of the song "Home," from the popular movie *The Wiz*, originally starring both Michael Jackson and Diana Ross.

SINGING ON SUNDAYS

On Sundays, the Knowleses attended services together at St. John's United Methodist Church, a home away from home for many families in the neighborhood. The congregation began with only nine members and, over the years, grew to thousands.

Pastors Rudy and Juanita, along with members of the congregation, supported young Beyoncé by giving her a place to grow in her faith and use her talents. Each week the dance ministry performed choreographed routines to gospel music throughout the service—a favorite part of church for the young Knowles sisters.

Not long after her first talent show performance, Beyoncé asked her parents if she could join the children's choir at St. John's. She loved the tone of the music and how the songs brought the whole congregation together.

⊰ WORKING WITH DAVID ⊱

In 1989, to help eight-year-old Beyoncé improve as a singer, the Knowles family hired David Lee Brewer, a graduate student at the Cleveland Institute of Music in Cleveland, Ohio. Tina had watched one of his performances and, after the show, asked David if he was willing to work with Beyoncé. David agreed to hear Beyoncé sing and was blown away by her skill. "Something about it grabbed me and wouldn't let go," he later said about her voice.

He accepted Beyoncé as one of his first clients and quickly realized he was teaching a star! As her voice coach, he wanted to give her an understanding of musical theory in addition to teaching practical techniques to improve her voice. David helped Beyoncé perfect her mezzo-soprano range, the most common range for female vocalists (see page 47).

Brewer considered Beyoncé to be a prodigy, a young person who has exceptional abilities. He decided to move into the Knowles home to be able to work around Beyoncé's school schedule, and he lived with the family for several years. He remembers her waking up every morning asking, "What am I going to learn today?"

As Beyoncé's confidence grew, her talent show wins kept on coming. Darlette entered her star student in several local contests, challenging the young girl to work harder.

"I put her in some singing and dancing competitions, and it's been history ever since. When I heard her sing for the first time, I knew she was special."
—Darlette Johnson

CHAPTER 2

A KNOWLES FAMILY AFFAIR

Sitting in the audience during one of Beyoncé's performances were two talent scouts, Denise Seals and Deborah Laday. They were creating a new group and were on the hunt for skilled young singers to audition. Impressed by Beyoncé's powerful vocals, they approached Mathew and Tina to ask whether their daughter was interested in trying out. Mathew was sure Beyoncé was ready for the next step and agreed to take her along to audition.

Although she was a confident performer, Beyoncé had never sung in a professional singing group before, and the idea was nerve-racking. On audition day at Evelyn Rubenstein Jewish Community Center, she entered the waiting room, packed with girls getting ready to sing.

⇃ WORKING HARD ⇂

One by one, the girls went up in front of Deborah
and Denise to audition for a group called Girls Tyme.
Beyoncé gave her performance everything she had,
then waited to hear the verdict. Would it be enough?
Finally, once everyone in the room had sung, Denise
and Deborah read out a list of names.

"Beyoncé!" they called. "You're in." She had made it!
One of the other successful girls was LaTavia Roberson,
a young singer whom Denise and Deborah had worked
with previously. The group began practicing right
away. On several evenings each week, Mathew or Tina
dropped Beyoncé off at Denise and Deborah's office.
There, the girls learned techniques for strengthening
their voices and creating harmonies. They began
performing at small venues around Houston and
auditioning for music showcases and TV commercials.

An investor named Andretta "Ann" Tillman
watched one of their performances and thought
that the group had serious potential. She offered
financial backing but wanted to make a few changes
to the lineup and to hire professional producer and
songwriter Lonnie Jackson.

Over the next few months, Denise, Deborah, Andretta, and Lonnie cut some of the singers from Girls Tyme and brought others in. The group grew to include Kelendria "Kelly" Rowland, a talented singer and friend of LaTavia's who had recently moved to Texas from Georgia. Kelly's father had fought in the Vietnam War and struggled with post-traumatic stress disorder, a mental health condition usually triggered by a stressful event. The strain on the family had led Kelly's mother to move to Texas in search of a fresh start. Like Beyoncé, Kelly was an amazing singer, but shy. The two girls hit it off at once.

Girls Tyme Members

Name: Beyoncé Knowles

Date of birth: September 4, 1981

Time with Girls Tyme: Beyoncé quickly picked up new lyrics and tricky harmonies, and was the lead singer of the group.

Name: Kelly Rowland

Date of birth: February 11, 1981

Time with Girls Tyme: After LaTavia encouraged her to audition, Kelly impressed Denise and Deborah with her rendition of "I'm Your Baby Tonight" by Whitney Houston.

Name: LaTavia Roberson

Date of birth: November 1, 1981

Time with Girls Tyme: LaTavia's big personality and stage presence made her a confident performer.

Name: Ashley Támar Davis

Date of birth: March 31, 1980

Time with Girls Tyme: Ashley left Girls Tyme because her parents wanted a more normal upbringing for her. She became a backup vocalist for Prince, which led to a solo career, a Grammy nomination, and an audition for the television singing competition show *The Voice*.

Performing in a group was very different from standing onstage alone. Now Beyoncé had to be sensitive to the movements of her bandmates and work on complicated harmonies. Almost every day, the girls headed to practice as soon as school was over and sometimes rehearsed late into the night.

During school breaks, Girls Tyme sang and danced all day long—even through the hot Texas summer. The Knowles family's living room became the main rehearsal space, but Mathew and

Tina also built a deck on the back of the house to create a stage for the girls.

When guests came over, the girls sometimes charged a small admission fee and then put on a show!

MOVING ON

In 1990, at age nine, Beyoncé transferred to Parker Elementary School, a school that specialized in music and performance. Studying music was easy, but Beyoncé still struggled with some of the other subjects. When teachers asked the class a question, Beyoncé felt like hiding. Even when she knew the answers, she didn't like the idea of walking up to the blackboard at the front of the room with her classmates' eyes on her.

But Beyoncé tried not to let her troubles at school affect her performances. Mathew and Tina spread the word about Girls Tyme, encouraging friends at church and work to go and watch the shows.

Sibling Rivalry?

Solange loved music, too, and Beyoncé often heard her little sister tinkering on a drum set in her bedroom next door. To make sure Beyoncé and Solange got along, Tina routinely took her daughters to see a child therapist to help them maintain their healthy relationship. Child therapists work with children and parents to address and treat any social, emotional, or developmental issues.

HEADLINERS SALON

Tina offered her salon to the girls as a rehearsal studio. With many of the customers sitting stiffly with their hair in rollers, Girls Tyme literally had a captive audience! Headliners, located on Montrose Boulevard, became a second home for the group, and many of Tina's customers became like family. Girls Tyme performed there so often that the stylists had their routines memorized. At the end of each performance, the customers clapped, and a few even asked for photos and autographs.

Mathew requested honest feedback from his wife's clients. In general, they were very positive, but sometimes they rolled their eyes and sighed as Girls Tyme got ready to perform yet another song!

"In the South in general, but specifically in our world growing up, people were expressive and vivid storytellers. In the hair salon or in the line at the grocery store, there was never a dull moment." —Solange

$\geq$ STAR SEARCH SORROW $\leq$

In 1992, all their salon rehearsals and local shows paid off when music producer Arne Frager saw the girls perform. Impressed by their talent, he flew the group out to California to professionally record some music in a studio. Beyoncé had never been on a plane before, and she enjoyed the three-hour flight.

The girls recorded a new track titled "Sunshine." Arne had high hopes of getting them signed by a major record label, but first he wanted them to have more exposure— on television. He got them booked for a spot on *Star Search*, a popular TV talent show. The girls were both terrified and excited at the prospect of performing on TV. They pushed their rehearsals into high gear, learning complicated choreography, practicing a rap song, and nailing their transitions around the stage.

Mathew was taking on more and more of the band's management, and rehearsals could be tense. During one practice, LaTavia missed a note, and all the other girls burst out laughing. Mathew didn't think the mishap was funny. He angrily told the girls that they needed to do better. Even though their next rendition of the song was pitch-perfect, his yelling had spoiled the mood.

Star Search

Star Search was a national television show hosted by Ed McMahon from the mid-1980s to the mid-1990s. Singers, dancers, actors, and comedians took to the stage to show off their talents. Many of the show's performers used the competition as a stepping-stone to getting record deals. Some of the biggest names in the music industry made their debuts on *Star Search*, including:

→ Justin Timberlake

→ Britney Spears

→ Christina Aguilera

→ LeAnn Rimes

→ Aaliyah

→ Usher

Backstage, the girls were so nervous they could hardly speak. This was the largest crowd Beyoncé had seen since Michael Jackson's concert, and there would be even more people watching on their televisions at home! They stepped onto the stage, dressed in green, purple, and white, and lined up like soldiers heading off to war. Beyoncé focused on the lyrics and made sure to stay in step with the others. The music came to a stop, and Girls Tyme hit their final pose. When the audience cheered loudly, the girls thought they had the top spot in the bag. Beyoncé was sure they were about to win *Star Search* and get signed by a major record label.

But instead, an adult rock and jazz band, Skeleton Crew, won that night. The members of Girls Tyme were incredibly disappointed, but the experience taught them an important lesson. Beyoncé realized that "you could actually work super hard and give everything you have and still lose." She also thought that the group had chosen the wrong song—they were singers, not rappers, and their performance had not demonstrated their skills.

"That was my first time I lost something that I really wanted to win." —Beyoncé

Even though Girls Tyme hadn't won, Mathew was proud of the girls for trying. Since they were in Florida, he took the whole group to Disney World. They got to ride roller coasters, eat candy, play games, and try to forget their disappointment. When the episode aired later that year, the girls were sad again, but watching their performance gave them another opportunity to critique their mistakes and make changes. Throughout her career, Beyoncé was sure to watch recordings of every performance; she always strove to improve her routines and avoid making the same mistake twice.

⌇ ALTERNATIVE SCHOOLING ⌇

Though Beyoncé had become close with the other members of Girls Tyme, her parents were worried that she still wasn't making friends at school. They wanted her to learn in a more supportive environment, so in eighth grade Beyoncé transferred to Welch Middle School.

Unfortunately, her experience wasn't much better than at Parker. Her grades weren't improving, and even though Beyoncé tried to keep her head down, some of the other students decided they just didn't like her. Her cousin Angie thought that they might be jealous of her looks—she even suggested they might try to cut Beyoncé's long hair—so Beyoncé wore it tied up for months. Though she was still quiet and timid at school, onstage she created an alter ego. Angie named this persona:

SASHA FIERCE

Sasha had a loud and boisterous personality. None of Beyoncé's classmates knew about Sasha, but this secret alter ego gave her courage.

Her parents understood that their daughter was having a difficult time at Welch and arranged for a private tutor to come to their house and help with her academic studies. When Beyoncé met Miss Little, her new tutor, she thought that she was strict and that the work she assigned was too hard. Beyoncé wanted to become a musician, not a mathematician, and she quickly became annoyed by Miss Little's frustrating teaching methods. Still, Beyoncé knew that Miss Little and her parents just wanted her to succeed, so she settled down and tried to get her head around the topics she was struggling with.

MANAGING GIRLS TYME

In 1992, Mathew started an entertainment company called Music World Entertainment. After Girls Tyme's disappointing performance on *Star Search,* he wanted to take over the management of the group. Denise and Deborah had already moved on to other projects, and Andretta was struggling with ill health. She agreed to hand over the reins. He scaled Girls Tyme back to four members: Kelly, LaTavia, Beyoncé, and a new member named LeToya.

BEYONCÉ
- powerful, soulful tone
- confident performer

KELLY ROWLAND
- broad vocal range, which worked well on upbeat songs

LATAVIA ROBERSON
- rich tone
- ability to hit the lowest notes

LETOYA LUCKETT
- ability to reach the highest notes

Voice Types

Most singers fit into a category, or "voice type," that reflects their vocal range. These include:

- **Soprano:** the highest voice type for females
- **Mezzo-soprano:** the most common type of female voice, falling between the high soprano and low alto
- **Contralto or alto:** the lowest voice type for females
- **Tenor:** the highest voice type for males, with the exception of the rare "countertenor" voice type, which is even higher
- **Baritone:** the most common type of male voice, falling between the high tenor range and the low bass range
- **Bass:** the lowest voice type for males

Each of the remaining members of Girls Tyme signed contracts with Music World Entertainment. At first things ran smoothly. Mathew made sure they were booked for shows and rehearsed for hours each day. Tina created custom costumes. Each girl had her own individual style, but the group always looked like a unit when they arrived at shows in sparkling fitted tops or brightly colored matching jumpsuits.

Kelly's mother worked long hours as a nanny, and it was becoming impossible to keep up with her daughter's daily practices. The decision was made that Kelly would move in with the Knowles family in order to give her full attention to Girls Tyme. The girls grew even closer, practicing through the day and having slumber parties at night.

BATTLE OF THE BANDS

For a short time, Beyoncé enrolled in Kinder High School for the Visual and Performing Arts. Once again, she enjoyed music classes but felt all other subjects were a distraction.

However, one of the things Beyoncé enjoyed about Kinder was attending the battle-of-the-bands competitions at nearby universities. At these events, marching bands played popular music and paraded around the university's grounds. Beyoncé dreamed of one day being among them and had future plans to attend Prairie View A&M University or Texas Southern University in Houston. Although she never made it to college, these events would go on to inspire one of her most iconic performances.

⋛ A RISING TENSION ⋛

A couple of the girls struggled with the fact that Mathew seemed to be able to dish out criticism but couldn't take it. If any of the band members complained about his management style or harsh comments, they felt like he disregarded their points and refused to acknowledge his faults.

"Mathew did not mince his words, and it can be tough to take that kind of criticism when you are a little girl. We would try not to let it break us."
—LaTavia Roberson

It was a trying time for Mathew and Tina as well. The two began arguing a lot and couldn't see eye to eye on Mathew's business decisions. To take on the group, he had quit his job at Xerox, swapped their large family home for a small apartment, and sold two of their three cars. "I felt like the group was more important to him than his family," Tina said. The tension continued to build, and when Beyoncé was twelve, they decided to spend some time apart.

During a six-month break from their marriage, Mathew moved out of their apartment and went to college to take a music management course. Tina worked overtime at the salon to support the family. The fracture was stressful for the girls. "It was such a painful time that I erased a lot of those memories from my head," Beyoncé said.

⋝ DESTINY'S CHILD ⋜

The stakes were high. The Knowles family invested everything they had in the success of their girl group. When summer hit, Mathew created a "boot camp" in the local park. He made the girls run laps around the track, singing, so that they didn't get out of breath while performing onstage. He had them practice dance routines in high heels, and he discouraged them from attending social events. On one occasion, he publicly scolded the girls mid-performance for going swimming the day before and damaging their voices.

Over the next few years, Mathew worked hard to make the girls successful, trying to book them as support artists for more established acts. Finally, they landed an audition with the record label Elektra.

They wowed the executives with their slick performance and were offered representation. It seemed like the big break they had all been waiting for! They spent the summer at a studio in Atlanta, missing months of school to record their tracks. But at the last minute, Elektra dropped the band. They'd decided the girls were "too young" to progress.

Beyoncé was crushed, as was Mathew. He decided the band needed a more mature image; the name Girls Tyme was now too young for them. The group went through several name changes, including Cliché, Something Fresh, and Da Dolls. Inspiration finally struck one evening when Tina opened her Bible and a photo of the girls fell out. On the page it had been holding, Tina read the word *destiny* in a passage in Isaiah, a book in the Old Testament. The girls felt like the word was a perfect fit, and added *child* to differentiate the group from others with similar names.

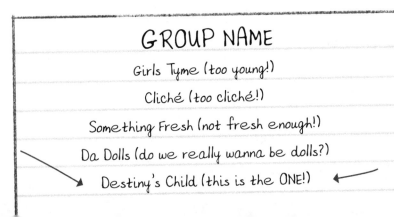

GROUP NAME

Girls Tyme (too young!)

Cliché (too cliché!)

Something Fresh (not fresh enough!)

Da Dolls (do we really wanna be dolls?)

→ Destiny's Child (this is the ONE!) ←

⋚ GETTING SIGNED ⋚

In 1997, the girls were offered an audition for
Columbia Records. The audition room was so tiny
that only the four singers could squeeze in and there
was no room for instruments. Beyoncé gave the
performance everything she had. Then the group
returned to Houston to wait for news.

A few weeks later, when the girls were gathered in
Headliners, Tina handed Beyoncé an envelope with
a local diner's logo emblazoned on the front. Thinking
her mother was giving her some gift certificates,
Beyoncé opened the envelope, only to discover a
letter from Columbia Records. Destiny's Child had
been signed!

CONTRACT

COLUMBIA RECORDS
DESTINY'S CHILD

Record Companies

A record company, often called a record label, is an organization that makes and sells musical recordings. The company helps musicians with their sound and image, maintains contracts, and markets their music by sending it out to influential distributors, magazines, and websites. The term *record label* comes from the circular label in the center of vinyl records, which displays the manufacturer's details.

CHAPTER 3

UNCHARTED WATERS

A few months after they were signed by Columbia, Destiny's Child's released its first song, "Killing Time." It was featured in *Men in Black*, a sci-fi film starring Will Smith, and word began to spread about the new girl band. Their record label encouraged Beyoncé, Kelly, LaTavia, and LeToya to pretend to be a couple of years older than they were, in order to appeal to a wider audience. When their second single, "No, No, No," charted at number three on *Billboard*'s Hot 100 in the United States, Columbia Records knew they had made a good decision in signing the group.

Record Charts

The main record chart in the
United States is published
weekly by *Billboard* magazine.
To calculate a song ranking,
Billboard takes into account
the number of sales, the number
of downloads, and the number of
times the song has been played
on the radio. It's difficult
to estimate the sales needed
for a single to reach the
chart, because the position is
determined by so many different
factors, including how well other
artists are performing that week.

Reaching gold, platinum, or even
multi-platinum is the ultimate
goal for many artists in the
music industry. To reach gold, an
album has to sell 500,000 copies;
platinum, 1 million copies; and
multi-platinum, 2 million copies.

ON THE RISE

One afternoon Beyoncé and Kelly were driving along, listening to a popular Houston radio station, when "No, No, No" started playing through the speakers. They turned up the volume as loud as it would go and belted out the lyrics. The girls celebrated all the way home—it would be the first of thousands of times their music was played on the radio.

Things were looking up in Beyoncé's personal life, too. Mathew and Tina had managed to settle their differences, and her father moved back into the family home.

As the band started work on its first album, Mathew wanted all the girls to be involved in the songwriting process. Beyoncé enjoyed putting together lyrics, and much of her inspiration came from conversations about love and heartbreak that she overheard at Headliners.

"Women in a hair salon are more open than men in a barbershop."
—Beyoncé

One year later, in 1998, Destiny's Child released its first album, a mix of romantic ballads and dance tunes. The album, called *Destiny's Child*, sold half a million copies within the first few weeks—not enough to set the world alight, but enough to encourage the group that they were on the right track. Their album release was followed by a few months of performances and a tour supporting Boyz II Men, one of the biggest R&B bands in the country. From Nashville to Los Angeles, Seattle to Washington, DC, the girls sang at a new venue most nights, before setting off on their tour bus for the next city the following morning. Though the tour was exhausting, Beyoncé enjoyed staying at fancy hotels and ordering room service with her friends every night.

The next year the girls joined R&B group TLC on tour as an opening act, and Destiny's Child carefully selected three of its most popular songs to perform: "Independent Women," "No, No, No," and "Jumpin', Jumpin'." On the night of their first performance in Toronto, Canada, as the bands waited backstage, Beyoncé walked up to TLC band members T-Boz, Left Eye, and Chilli to thank them for "one of the best times" in her life. They formed a circle and prayed together before Destiny's Child strutted onto the stage, ready to perform in front of the roaring crowd.

After each performance, there was a meet-and-greet with fans. With the final autographs signed and pictures taken, the girls spent time together on their tour bus, snacking on junk food and gossiping about the show. The beds were stacked on top of each other like Legos, but the teens didn't mind. To them, it felt like a fun slumber party every night.

⋛ THE WRITING'S ON THE WALL ⋛

In 1999, Destiny's Child recorded a second album, *The Writing's on the Wall*. In this collection, Beyoncé's lyrics got more personal, and many of the songs focused on empowering women or finding love. She sang the lead vocals on most of the tracks, occasionally sharing them with Kelly. LaTavia and LeToya generally sang the backing vocals, but sometimes Beyoncé or Kelly recorded those parts, too.

LaTavia and LeToya disagreed with Mathew's management style and felt that Beyoncé and Kelly got more time in the spotlight, while they were left in the background. To them, it felt like there was a clear divide between the group members who lived in the Knowles family home and those who didn't. Onstage, LaTavia and LeToya felt they were always in the shadow of the other singers, given fewer solos, and positioned at the back during the dance routines. The two claimed Mathew wasn't looking out for all the girls' best interests, and they demanded answers from him. Rehearsals became tense, especially when nothing seemed to change regarding who was landing the big solos or best stage positions.

But LaTavia and LeToya continued to struggle. They called all of the girls together and suggested that they consider new management—they wanted Mathew out. Beyoncé and Kelly were happy with Mathew, and they trusted his judgment. It seemed they were at an impasse.

LaTavia and LeToya contacted a mediator, someone who could talk business on their behalf. LaTavia's mother, who chaperoned the girls at times, didn't agree with the decision to seek outside advice, but the girls proceeded anyway. Beyoncé and Kelly didn't want to be involved. They loved LaTavia and LeToya, but were comfortable letting Mathew handle the business side of things, so they could remain focused on the music.

When Destiny's Child's next single was released, LaTavia and LeToya noticed that their vocals weren't on the track. They had recorded "Say My Name" along with Beyoncé and Kelly in the studio, but Mathew had decided to find new singers, Michelle Williams and Farrah Franklin, to record over their parts.

LaTavia and LeToya felt they were being punished for voicing their concerns and filed a lawsuit against Mathew for breaching their contract. They reached a settlement before the case went to court, and both girls were awarded thousands of dollars in compensation. There are differing accounts of the circumstances that led to their departure, but however it happened, LaTavia and LeToya were out, and Michelle and Farrah in.

"Say My Name" was the group's biggest hit so far. It won Destiny's Child its first two Grammys and stayed on the charts for an impressive thirty-two weeks. Still, Beyoncé's happiness at their hard-won success was dampened as tabloid newspapers and gossip websites blamed her for the issues within the group. Upset by this negative publicity, she withdrew from her family and friends and struggled to come to terms with the dark side of fame.

Beyoncé sometimes faced bouts of intense sadness she couldn't explain. There were even days when she had difficulty leaving her bedroom. With therapy and support, Beyoncé found ways to cope with her depression while on the road, and music became an outlet in her lowest moments.

"I didn't eat. I stayed in my room. I was in a really bad place in life."
—Beyoncé

Depression

Depression is a mood disorder. It causes symptoms that negatively affect your thoughts and feelings. Often, people with depression have a difficult time performing common daily tasks, like eating, working, and socializing. People who experience these or other symptoms of depression should talk to a doctor or other health care provider. Symptoms include:

- Feeling sad
- Feeling extremely tired
- Lacking concentration
- Losing interest in activities you used to enjoy
- Sleeping less or more than usual
- Feeling irritable or grumpy
- Feeling guilty

A NEW LINEUP

After just five months with the band, Farrah left Destiny's Child. The exact reason for her swift departure is unknown. Some sources suggest that Farrah missed one too many practices and was dismissed from the group, while others state that she disagreed with Mathew's management style and left of her own accord. Either way, the quartet was down to a trio.

The shakeup was a shift in the chemistry at first. The four original members had been close friends, constantly together, but it didn't take long for the trio to adjust to the new group dynamic. Beyoncé and Kelly welcomed Michelle and helped her catch up with the choreography. They started rehearsing new music straightaway, and their voices sounded like magic together. This was a new opportunity to reinvent themselves.

"It's been wonderful. In two weeks, we were shooting the 'Say My Name' video. We've been shooting up toward the sky ever since." —Michelle Williams

Michelle Williams

Born July 23, 1980, Michelle loved music from a young age. When she was seven years old, she sang "Blessed Assurance" in front of her entire church congregation. Unlike Beyoncé, Michelle wasn't always sure she wanted to be a professional singer, so she attended Illinois State University to study criminal justice, but she left before she graduated to turn her attention back to the music industry. Before joining Beyoncé and Kelly, Michelle provided backing vocals for R&B singer Monica.

STUDIO SESSIONS

When recording at the studio, Beyoncé, Kelly, and Michelle took turns reading lyrics, practicing refrains, and offering each other critiques. Beyoncé in particular took an interest in the technical side of things—she wanted to understand what sounded good and how to make it happen. Sometimes, they sang one phrase over and over again until it was just right. In 2000, their new single "Independent Women" shot straight to the top of the *Billboard* charts for eleven consecutive weeks, setting a record for the longest-running number one song by a girl group.

SURVIVOR

In 2001, Beyoncé, Kelly, and Michelle visited a radio station. Live on air, the show's host teased the girls about who would be leaving next. The host compared their group to the television show *Survivor*, where contestants live on a deserted island, with one member voted off each week. With Farrah's dismissal still fresh, the joke hit too close to home. Destiny's Child wanted to present like a strong, solid family, and digs about their instability stung. But rather than let it get her down, Beyoncé used the snide joke as inspiration for one of the group's biggest hit songs, "Survivor." She put a positive spin on a negative comment, coming up with the powerful lyrics: "I'm a survivor, I'm not gon' give up, I'm not gon' stop, I'm gon' work harder."

When Columbia Records released Destiny's Child's third album, *Survivor*, on May 1, 2001, it debuted at number one on the *Billboard* chart. In just the first week of its release, the album sold 663,000 copies!

Oops!

During the filming of the "Survivor" video, Beyoncé and the rest of the group were put to the test. Temperatures were at a record low in Los Angeles, but the video shoot called for a beach scene. That meant they had to brave the cold and step into the forty-degree water. They were so chilly that it was hard to keep their teeth from chattering when they were singing! They tried to make the best of the day and even enjoyed a few laughs. When a helicopter flew too low, Kelly's wig flew off, sending all three members running along the beach to retrieve it!

CHAPTER 4

OFF THE CHARTS

Destiny's Child earned a Grammy for "Survivor," but some of the messages in the lyrics caused a stir, and LaTavia and LeToya took offense at lines such as:

"Now that you're outta my life, I'm so much better"
and
"Thought I wouldn't sell without you,
sold nine million."

They filed another lawsuit, arguing that the song was disparaging, and that it should never be played again. Many people thought that the lawsuit would be the end of Destiny's Child, but it was eventually settled quietly, with all parties coming to an agreement. It was another difficult time for Beyoncé, as once again many journalists pointed fingers in her direction, blaming her for causing the drama.

⹀ BOOTYLICIOUS ⹀

Not long after the release of "Survivor," Destiny's
Child was on a long plane flight to London, when
the word *bootylicious* popped into Beyoncé's
head. She began scribbling down lyrics, writing
a song that celebrated full-figured woman and
encouraged all women to embrace their body sizes.
She apprehensively shared her song with the other
members. Kelly and Michelle loved the concept, and
later in 2001 the girls released their hit single.

Over the following years, the term *bootylicious*
became so commonly used that in 2004 the *Oxford
English Dictionary* added the word.

*I don't think you're ready
for this
'Cause my body's too bootylicious
for ya, babe*

Destiny's Child was invited to open the Seventh Annual Soul Train Lady of Soul Awards at the Santa Monica Civic Auditorium. Although the event was usually a celebration, the night Destiny's Child opened the show, there was a somber feeling lingering in the air. Just a few days before, on August 25, 2001, after shooting a music video, twenty-two-year-old R&B singer Aaliyah boarded a flight in the Bahamas but never made it off the island. The plane crashed and caught fire near the runway. The pilot and all nine passengers, including Aaliyah, were killed.

Her presence was missed during the awards show. Beyoncé, Kelly, and Michelle sang "Emotion" to pay homage to Aaliyah, whose music touched some of the same fans.

"She was so sweet, always.
She was one of the most beautiful
people on the inside and out."
—Beyoncé

9/11 Attacks

On September 11, 2001, a terrorist group called al-Qaeda hijacked four passenger planes and deliberately crashed them into buildings. Two of the planes crashed into the Twin Towers of the World Trade Center in New York City; a third plane hit the Pentagon in Washington, DC. Passengers tried to retake control of the fourth plane from the hijackers, but it crashed in Shanksville, Pennsylvania. In total, 2,977 people were killed. The attack shocked the world and still raises strong emotions today.

⋛ NEW PROJECTS ⋚

After the September 11 attacks, Destiny's Child made the difficult decision to cancel the rest of its world tour on the grounds that it was too dangerous to travel at this time. Though she was devastated about letting her fans down, canceling the tour allowed Beyoncé time to try something new—acting.

Mathew presented her with a script for a TV movie, a hip-hop remake of *Carmen*, an 1875 Georges Bizet opera. The lead female character is an aspiring actress named Carmen, trying to make her way in Hollywood. Carmen uses her beauty and cunning to charm two men who should be off-limits to her. Beyoncé's interest was piqued; she liked the idea of acting, and the role would stretch her as an artist. Carmen was worldly and sly, whereas Beyoncé had a sheltered upbringing. She would need to dig deep to find her way into this character's head. Beyoncé attended auditions, then waited to hear if she had gotten the role.

Carmen: A Hip Hop...
CAST
CARMEN BROWN: Beyoncé

DEREK HILL: Mekhi Phi...

LT. MILLLER: Mos Def

RASHEEDA: Rah Digga

NIKKI: Joy Bryant

NARRATOR: Da Brat

A few weeks later, the call she had been hoping for came. The producers had decided Beyoncé was perfect for the role! Filming with seasoned actors was thrilling. Beyoncé liked getting to know her costars, as well as those working behind the scenes. Although she met lots of new people at every show with Destiny's Child, she never got to talk for long. A concert stop lasted only a few hours, and the singers were often rushed back onto their tour bus immediately after the performance. Beyoncé enjoyed spending time with the other young actors, even if she did feel very uncomfortable performing her first on-screen kiss!

Besides Kelly and Michelle, I'm not around people our age for more than forty-five minutes. So I was around people my age for a month and a half, and I made friends. So it was way more than a movie for me.

After the release of *Carmen: A Hip Hopera*, she continued searching for roles to help her grow as an artist. Over the next few years, she appeared in *Austin Powers in Goldmember* (2002) and *The Fighting Temptations* (2003).

AUSTIN POWERS IN GOLDMEMBER

CARMEN: A HIP HOPERA

THE FIGHTING TEMPTATIONS

In 2002, Destiny's Child set out on its first world tour. Everyone in the Knowles camp helped to prepare, including Beyoncé's younger sister. When one of the backup dancers had to leave the tour early, Solange, a classically trained ballet dancer, stepped in.

"She was and is such a role model, but I think more so it was an insane learning process for me to have a big sister like that—to be able to see the good, the bad, and everything in between that comes with fame and success, and to know what I was getting myself into." —Solange

No longer a small-town group, Destiny's Child had a list of requests for each venue, known as a rider:

Destiny's Child: Dressing Room Rider

- six bottles of iced tea
- fine china and dinnerware (no plastic cups)
- a selection of sodas
- chips and salsa
- fresh fruit
- deli tray (no pork)
- lemons, honey, and fresh ginger (VERY IMPORTANT)
- spring water
- fresh flowers
- soap and towels
- two strawberry candles

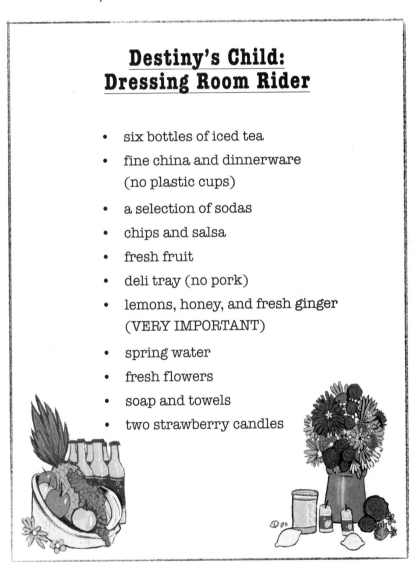

OUT OF THE SPOTLIGHT

Between creating new music, performing with Destiny's Child, and appearing in movies, Beyoncé was incredibly busy. However, she tried to get back to Houston as often as she could to spend time with her family and visit her childhood church.

Around this time, she became close to hip-hop artist Jay-Z. The two had met at various events over the previous few years and exchanged numbers at a photo shoot. Jay-Z was twelve years older than Beyoncé, but she liked him right from the start. Though Jay-Z was based in Fort Lee, New Jersey, over 1,600 miles away from Beyoncé's Houston home, the pair kept in regular contact and were soon calling each other every day. As they grew closer, Beyoncé and Jay-Z met up as often as their schedules allowed, and enjoyed going to movies together or simply hanging out and listening to music. Even as love blossomed, the couple was very private about the relationship and repeatedly denied that they were an item. Beyoncé didn't want the press speculating about her love life and was determined never to be photographed with Jay-Z.

Jay-Z

Rapper Jay-Z was born Shawn
Corey Carter in New York
City on December 4, 1969.
As a child in the Marcy
Houses, a housing project
in Brooklyn, he had trouble
focusing at school and got
involved with the local drug gangs.

To escape the dangerous street life,
Jay-Z started rapping, and in 1989 he
landed an appearance on the show *Yo!
MTV Raps*. Over the next seven years,
Jay-Z took the hip-hop world by storm,
releasing many number one albums. In
2004, he became president of Def Jam
Recordings and signed artists including
Rihanna and Ne-Yo.

"I never lost sense of who I was, not for
a day, not before I had a record deal,
and certainly not after." –Jay-Z

In 2002, Destiny's Child completed the tour that had been cut short the previous year. Fans screamed, danced, and sang along in every packed stadium. These were no longer the little girls who had failed to win *Star Search* but one of the bestselling groups of all time.

CHAPTER 5

DESTINY FULFILLED

Beyoncé, Kelly, and Michelle had worked tirelessly to reach the top of the charts, and by 2002 they were ready for a break. The members of Destiny's Child were all eager to take on individual projects. Fans worried that this might mean the end for Destiny's Child, but the record label reassured the public that the band wouldn't be splitting up, just taking some time to work on other things.

⌇ A NEW PARTNERSHIP ⌇

Jay-Z and Beyoncé released a single together, "'03 Bonnie and Clyde." On the track, Jay-Z sings, "All I need in this life of sin is me and my girlfriend," to which Beyoncé replies, "Down to ride till the very end, is me and my boyfriend." For some fans, this was confirmation enough that the two were dating.

But even with rumors swirling, Beyoncé and Jay-Z refused to confirm or deny that they were together. When asked about the nature of their relationship, Jay-Z told one reporter, "She's beautiful. Who wouldn't wish she was their girlfriend? Maybe one day."

<u>Bonnie and Clyde</u>

Jay-Z and Beyoncé's track was named after two infamous criminals who traveled the United States together in the 1930s. Bonnie and Clyde led police on a chase across the country, robbing several businesses and murdering 13 people. The two were finally tracked down by a Texas Ranger in Bienville Parish, Louisiana, where they were shot and killed.

INDEPENDENT WOMEN

In 2002, Michelle released *Heart to Yours*, a bestselling gospel album that reached the top of the *Billboard* Gospel Albums chart. The lyrics spoke of her faith and acknowledged victims of the September 11, 2001, attacks. Beyoncé and Kelly were featured as guest vocalists on one of the tracks, "Gospel Medley." Michelle won Best Gospel Act at the Music of Black Origin (MOBO) Awards and performed on Broadway.

On October 22, 2002, Kelly followed suit and released her own solo project, *Simply Deep*, a fusion of R&B and rock songs. The gold album featured appearances by artists Nelly, Solange, and Joe Budden. A year later, Kelly left for a three-week Simply Deeper Tour to promote the album.

"It was a challenge. . . . I was very nervous, but I came through with flying colors because of my family and, of course, Destiny's Child. There were days in the studio where I would run out." —Kelly Rowland

⋛ A SOLO ALBUM ⋛

Beyoncé was also working on a solo album. She invited a group of talented writers, including Dr. Dre and Jay-Z, to come together to share ideas. Beyoncé enjoyed collaboration; she listened intently to feedback and opinions about new styles to consider. When Beyoncé was introduced to song samples—initial recordings of a beat, melody, and lyrics—she listened to the tune several times, then rewrote the lyrics so that each line spoke to who she is as an artist.

Although Beyoncé has a hand in writing most of her songs, she has also worked with some of the biggest names in the industry, collaborating with such music greats as Timbaland, Missy Elliott, Rich Harrison, Jay-Z, Rockwilder, Swizz Beatz, Rodney Jerkins, and Mark Batson.

The team compiled forty-three songs, of which fifteen were selected by her record label for her solo album, *Dangerously in Love*. Columbia Records was lukewarm about the album and told Beyoncé's team they didn't think there was one big hit on the track list. It would turn out that there were four.

Out of the fifteen songs on the album, the four chart-topping songs were:
→ "Crazy in Love" (number one)
→ "Baby Boy" (number one)
→ "Me, Myself and I" (number four)
→ "Naughty Girl" (number three)

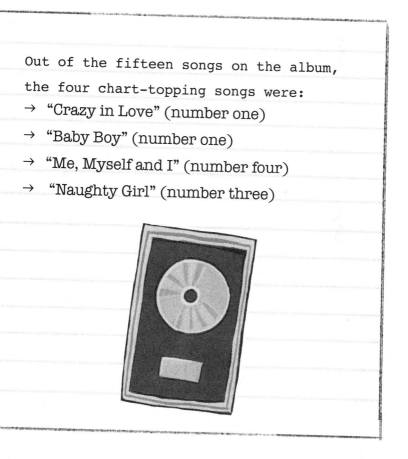

☰ SECRET SONG ☰

On June 23, 2003, *Dangerously in Love* shot right to the top of the *Billboard* charts, and "Crazy in Love" remained the number one single for eight weeks. With more than 10 million copies sold worldwide, Beyoncé was on her way to superstardom.

There was a surprise for Mathew on the album. Beyoncé had kept the last track a secret. It was titled "Daddy" and paid tribute to her father, speaking of their close bond.

You cure my disappointments
and you heal my pain
You understood my biz and
you protected me

Mathew was touched, but not everyone was such a fan of Beyoncé's father. There were rumors that he and Jay-Z didn't get along. It was reported that Jay-Z thought Mathew was too controlling, and Mathew resented Jay-Z's involvement in his daughter's work.

When the album was released, rumors circulated about hidden messages—could Beyoncé be confirming that she'd met someone special? And was that special person Jay-Z? He certainly featured in two of the tracks and had writing credits on four. In addition to making music together, the two artists modeled for the cover of fashion magazine *Vanity Fair*'s music issue. The public appearance fueled more romance rumors, but they still kept quiet on the subject.

Beyoncé was proud of what she had accomplished. In 2002, Beyoncé's talents were recognized when she became the first black woman to win the American Society of Composers, Authors, and Publishers (ASCAP) Pop Songwriter of the Year award, for "Independent Women Part I," "Jumpin', Jumpin'," and "Survivor."

New Nephew

On October 18, 2004, Daniel Julez J. Smith Jr. was born to parents Solange Knowles and her then partner, Daniel Smith. Beyoncé shares a close bond with her nephew, now known by his middle name, Julez, and babysat for him as often as her scheduled allowed when he was younger.

⋛ AN EMOTIONAL REUNION ⋜

The members of Destiny's Child reunited in 2004 to release *Destiny Fulfilled*. When the trio returned to the studio, they spent a full week chatting about their lives. There was a lot to catch up on—love, solo projects, and so much growth!

"The first couple of days we couldn't write anything. We couldn't do anything but talk and eat and laugh and clown. We had the best conversations, which actually became the concept and the theme of the albums. It's all about friendship and it's all about this journey." —Beyoncé

While they were catching up, one of the producers recorded some of their conversations. He felt that the raw, candid discussions would be a good opening for the *Destiny Fulfilled* album. All three group members had a hand in writing and producing the comeback album, and the vocals were fairly balanced, with no one singer dominating. Full of mid-tempo ballads and emotion-heavy pop songs, like "Lose My Breath," "Soldier," "Girl," and "Cater 2 U," the album received mixed reviews, but Beyoncé claimed it was more a celebration of their friendship than a musical statement. Besides, it still reached number two on the *Billboard* chart!

The following year, the trio took the Destiny Fulfilled show on the road. Long-time fans of the group were thrilled. The tour started in Hiroshima, Japan, on April 9, 2005, and ended in Vancouver, Canada, on September 10. They held more than sixty shows in Asia, Australia, and North America.

The tour was a huge success. Every leg of the final journey was sold out, the venues filled with fans who loved the group. But at one of their final shows, Kelly stepped forward to address the 60,000-strong crowd in the Barcelona, Spain, stadium:

We just wanna say that this Destiny Fulfilled tour has been so wonderful. . . .This is the last time that you'll see Michelle, Beyoncé, and myself onstage as Destiny's Child in Europe.

They were splitting up! As the last song ended at their final performance in Vancouver, Beyoncé, Kelly, and Michelle joined hands. When the crowd hushed enough for her to speak, Beyoncé addressed their fans:

"We don't want to get too mushy, y'all. Destiny's Child started when we were nine years old. This isn't something somebody put together. This is love." It was the end of an era.

DREAMGIRLS

Her time as the lead singer of Destiny's Child was over, but Beyoncé quickly began looking for new opportunities. In 2006, she appeared in *Dreamgirls*, a film based on the rise of popular 1960s group the Supremes. When Beyoncé read the script, she related to the character Deena, who is quiet and talented. Beyoncé knew she could bring Deena to life, but the director, Bill Condon, had someone else in mind for the role. Beyoncé had to complete a screen test to change his mind!

Throughout filming, Beyoncé paused on making her own music so that she could immerse herself in the sounds of the sixties. Though she felt "born for this role," taking on such an emotionally charged character left Beyoncé feeling drained. As with all her projects, she couldn't help giving everything she could to make the movie successful, even at the expense of her well-being.

For her performance, she was nominated for a Golden Globe Award for Best Original Song for "Listen," a power ballad about taking back control, along with a nomination for Best Actress: Motion Picture Comedy or Musical.

≡ COUTURE. KICK. SOUL. ≡

While she was working on *Dreamgirls*, Beyoncé was collaborating with her mother on a very different kind of project. She and Tina appeared on *The Oprah Winfrey Show* to introduce the House of Deréon, a ready-to-wear clothing and fashion line inspired by the style of three generations of women in their family. Deréon was Beyoncé's grandmother's maiden name.

Agnèz Deréon Beyincé

Agnèz taught herself to sew and worked as a seamstress for private clients throughout her life. She created unique designs, working with embellishments like embroidery, lace, and jeweled buttons. In order to make enough money for Catholic school for her children, Agnèz also made robes for altar boys.

The fashion line's tagline—"Couture. Kick. Soul."—was directly inspired by the three women. Tina was the couture, Beyoncé was the kick, and Agnèz was the soul. The clothes were hip, wearable, and unique. A couple of years later, Beyoncé and Solange launched a junior clothing line. Unusually for Beyoncé's projects, neither clothing line gained much commercial success, and she sold both companies after just a few years.

⋛ A POWER COUPLE ⋚

Slowly, Jay-Z and Beyoncé became more vocal about their relationship. Jay-Z was featured on a couple of songs on Beyoncé's next album, *B'Day*, released on September 4, 2006. He also released the single "Lost One" that year, in which he requested more attention from his girlfriend, rapping "I don't think it's meant to be, B. But she loves her work more than she does me."

This trend toward a more raw and open relationship with fans would continue over the next few years as Beyoncé explored new areas of music and established herself as the ultimate queen of the spotlight.

CHAPTER 6

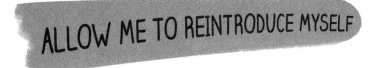

ALLOW ME TO REINTRODUCE MYSELF

Paparazzi and fans were watching Beyoncé's every move, with cameras flashing in her face whenever she left her home. The pressure to look perfect was overwhelming, and there were some parts of her life that she preferred not to share.

On April 4, 2008, Beyoncé and Jay-Z invited fewer than forty of their closest friends and family to his penthouse to witness their wedding vows. The space was decorated with seventy thousand white orchids that had been flown in from Thailand. The ceremony was top secret, and they had a rule for their guests: no cell phones allowed. They didn't want any photos from their private ceremony leaked to the papers or social media.

Rather than opt for an expensive designer dress, Beyoncé wore a strapless ivory wedding gown that Tina had created. The couple marked their special day with matching "IV" (the Roman numeral for "four") tattoos on their ring fingers.

The number four is special to Beyoncé and Jay-Z. They are both born on the fourth day of the month. They were married on the fourth day of the fourth month of the year. Beyoncé's fourth album, titled 4, was released on June 24.

Home, Sweet Home

Both Beyoncé and Jay-Z have owned or rented impressive property all over the United States, including these:

- Tribeca, New York (2004)
  Jay-Z's 8,000-square-foot penthouse had a large outdoor terrace and was the perfect spot for a small wedding to his bride, Beyoncé, in 2008.

- Midtown Manhattan, New York (2007)
  Jay-Z paid $40,000 per month for an unobstructed view of the magical Manhattan skyline from the 76th floor of the Time Warner Center building.

- Indian Creek Village, Florida (2008)
  After their wedding, the couple bought a compound on this exclusive piece of land. The home has seven bedrooms and eight bathrooms and is one of only 35 homes on the island.

TRIBECA, NEW YORK

- New Orleans, Louisiana (2015)

  Beyoncé bought this converted historic church with a mix of traditional and modern decor, along with a roof garden.

- Hamptons, New York (2017)

  Jay-Z and Beyoncé can escape to the peace and quiet of the Pond House, their 17-acre home less than two hours outside New York City.

- Los Angeles, California (2018)

  This $88 million property has six buildings, several pools, a basketball court, and separate staff quarters. It was the most expensive sale of 2017 in the whole of Los Angeles County!

LOS ANGELES, CALIFORNIA

SASHA FIERCE

On November 12, 2008, Beyoncé introduced the world to her alter ego with her third solo album, *I Am . . . Sasha Fierce*. It took eight months for her to co-write and coproduce the collection, and of the seventy songs she recorded, her label selected sixteen—eleven tracks for the standard edition and five more for the deluxe edition.

I Am . . . Sasha Fierce was released on two discs to make room for both of Beyoncé's personas. The "I Am" side featured softer, more emotional tracks, like "If I Were a Boy" and "Halo," while the "Sasha Fierce" side was livelier, with some of her biggest chart hits, including "Single Ladies." Despite her success as one of the greatest performers of all time, Beyoncé still felt shy. Sasha Fierce was the opposite, and Beyoncé wanted fans to understand that both personas were a part of her.

I wouldn't like Sasha if I met her offstage. . . . The people around me know who I really am.

I Am . . . Sasha Fierce debuted at number one, making it her third album to do so. It sold more than 8 million copies around the world, and the video for "Single Ladies" would go down in music history. Along with two other dancers, Beyoncé performed an iconic routine that inspired hundreds of copycats.

Cadillac Records

After her album's success, Beyoncé once again took to the big screen, this time to play Etta James in the film *Cadillac Records*. The movie is loosely based on the life of record company executive Leonard Chess, a Jewish man who created opportunities for black artists, including Etta James, during the 1950s. Unlike the role in *Dreamgirls*, Etta's part was written with Beyoncé in mind. She recorded five songs, including a cover of Etta's biggest hit, "At Last." Etta was pleased with her portrayal, and Beyoncé recalls her saying, "I loved you from the first time you sang."

⋝ FRIENDS IN HIGH PLACES ⋜

The same year, history was made with the election of the first black president of the United States. Both Beyoncé and Jay-Z were very vocal in their support of Barack Obama, whom Beyoncé called "the American dream," promoting his campaign at every opportunity and striking up a personal friendship with his family.

The following January, Beyoncé performed "At Last" at Obama's inauguration ball as the new president slow-danced with his wife, Michelle. Of all of Beyoncé's thousands of performances, this proved to be one of the most emotional, and she struggled to hold back tears.

Barack Obama

Barack Obama was born in Honolulu, Hawaii, on August 4, 1961. He was raised by his mother and his grandparents before attending Occidental College in Los Angeles and Columbia University in New York City. He went on to study at Harvard Law School and became the first person of African American heritage to serve as editor of the *Harvard Law Review*. In 2008, he was elected president of the United States.

⋛ A BIG NIGHT ⋛

On January 31, 2010, at the Fifty-Second Annual Grammy Awards, Beyoncé's *I Am . . . Sasha Fierce* was nominated for Album of the Year, bringing her total number of nominations to ten. It was a star-studded night, and she was surrounded by the best artists in the business, including Elton John, Celine Dion, and Bon Jovi.

This was one of the biggest moments in her career. She ended the night by earning six Grammys, the most ever won by a female artist in a single night, a record that would be matched by Adele two years later.

⊰ GIVING BACK ⊱

With her fame and success came fortune, and
Beyoncé wanted to give back to the community.
Throughout her career, she'd donated vast sums of
money to various causes and been heavily involved in
numerous charity projects. Alongside Kelly Rowland,
she'd started the Survivor Foundation, an organization
that supported victims of Hurricane Katrina, in 2005.

In 2010, Beyoncé and her mother, Tina, opened
the Beyoncé Cosmetology Center at the Phoenix
House Career Academy in Brooklyn, where
recovering drug users could train to become
hairdressers and beauticians. The singer learned
about the work happening at Phoenix House while

researching her role as Etta
James, who'd struggled
with addiction. Beyoncé
hoped to bring a little of the
community spirit that she
had found at Headliners to
these men and women who
were struggling to get their
lives back on track.

⋜ ARTIST OF THE MILLENNIUM ⋜

In 2011, Beyoncé cut ties with Mathew as her manager.
She told the media this was purely a business decision—
as Mathew described it, "Business is business and family
is family." Despite repeatedly stating that they were
fine, Beyoncé later admitted that going their separate
ways professionally had put a strain on their personal
relationship. Around this time, Mathew and Tina, who
had been living apart for several years, decided to
officially divorce, further distancing Beyoncé from
her father.

But it wasn't all doom and gloom. With her newfound creative freedom, Beyoncé began work on her ambitious fourth studio album, aptly titled *4*. The video for one of the biggest hits on the album, "Run the World (Girls)," saw Beyoncé performing a routine alongside two Mozambican dancers. She had come across a YouTube clip of the dancers' troupe over a year before and admired their relaxed rhythmic style.

She'd asked her team to invite the dancers to the United States to help choreograph her video and to teach Beyoncé's backup dancers their technique. It took months to track down the group, but eventually they were found and brought to Beyoncé's studio.

Though excited by the opportunity, it appeared the group didn't quite grasp how influential their host was. "What's your name?" asked one of the dancers when he was introduced to the international superstar. "I'm Beyoncé," the singer replied, smiling humbly and shaking his hand. Rehearsals quickly got underway. The dance group brought a new energy to the set, and Beyoncé was reminded of her fifteen-year-old self, shooting her own first music video.

Her efforts were well rewarded when, in 2011, *Billboard* magazine gave Beyoncé the *Billboard* Millennium Award during the *Billboard* Music Awards show in Las Vegas, Nevada, on May 22. Beyoncé wore a long sparkling gown and performed "Run the World (Girls)" on television for the first time. To top off an already special night, Tina and Julez presented her with the award. Onstage, Beyoncé hugged her mom and nephew and thanked Kelly, Michelle, Jay-Z, and even previous Destiny's Child members LaTavia and LeToya.

⋛ STARTING A FAMILY ⋛

Though Beyoncé and Jay-Z were ready to expand their family, it would prove more difficult than the two had planned. When Beyoncé became pregnant, the couple was thrilled, but their excitement was short lived. During a check-up with her doctor, Beyoncé learned that she'd had a miscarriage.

But in 2011, at MTV's Video Music Awards, Beyoncé had happier news to share. Dressed in a white button-up shirt and purple spangled jacket, she walked onto the stage to give her fans a surprise.

"Tonight I want you to stand up on your feet. I want you to feel the love that's growing inside of me." —Beyoncé

When her performance of "Love on Top" had ended, she smiled, pulled open her blazer, and rubbed her baby bump. She was pregnant!

With her pregnancy announcement, Beyoncé nearly broke Twitter! In response to her news, there were almost 9,000 tweets per second.

On January 7, 2012, Beyoncé started feeling contractions and headed to the hospital in New York City. The couple welcomed a daughter to the world and named her Blue Ivy, a play on words, as *Ivy* sounds like "IV," the Roman numeral for their favorite number.

CHAPTER 7

ON THE RUN

Beyoncé took to motherhood the way she had taken to every other challenge in her life. She adored spending time with her daughter, who she thought was the most amazing thing she had ever created. But soon she felt the itch to get back in the studio and on the stage.

If there was any doubt that Beyoncé had established herself as an iconic artist, she dispelled it in 2013 with one of the most memorable Super Bowl performances of all time. In some ways, the grueling eight-hundred-second set was a culmination of everything she had ever worked toward, bringing together her impressive list of chart-topping hits with fantastic staging and slick choreography.

"I'm a perfectionist," Beyoncé admitted to a journalist, discussing the five months of intense rehearsals during which she'd often finish practice in the early hours of the morning, her feet bloodied and bruised.

Every part of the performance had to be exactly right, from the backup dancers to the lighting. Her outfit, a tight black bodysuit, took two hundred hours to put together. Due to the intense rehearsal schedule, Beyoncé lost weight, and the waist had to be taken in repeatedly to ensure a flattering fit.

The set began with an explosion of red-and-white flares and a giant white outline of Beyoncé above the stage. Then the singer emerged to perform "Love on Top." Later, Beyoncé was joined by Michelle and Kelly, who rose up through hidden trapdoors to sing a few of Destiny's Child's greatest hits to the 70,000-strong crowd. To wrap up the performance, Beyoncé turned down the tempo and ended on the emotionally charged "Halo."

The set went down in history. The *New York Times* declared that Beyoncé had "silenced her doubters," and the British newspaper the *Daily Telegraph* called it a "take-no-prisoners assault on the senses." Moments after she had finished, a power outage in the stadium caused a delay to the second half. For many, Bey's performance had literally overshadowed the game.

The Super Bowl Halftime Show

The Super Bowl is one of the most-watched events on television, and the halftime show provides an opportunity for legendary musicians to reach an audience of millions.

One of the most memorable halftime performances was Michael Jackson's headlining set during Super Bowl XXVII. A few years after her first appearance, Beyoncé played homage to Michael's iconic black-and-gold military-style outfit during her politically charged 2016 Super Bowl performance of "Formation."

SUPER BOWL

It wasn't long before Beyoncé was once again sharing new music, with the surprise release of her fifth album, *Beyoncé*, in 2013. Even though there had been no announcement or advertising, the album sold a million copies worldwide in just six days! Beyoncé showcased a different, edgier sound, and she recorded an intimate music video for each song, showing many different sides of herself, in her roles as a new mother, a professional entertainer, and a businesswoman.

In the video for "Pretty Hurts," Beyoncé competes in a beauty pageant, wearing a sash that reads *Miss 3rd Ward*, a reference to the numerous competitions she entered as a child.

⸗ AROUND THE GLOBE AGAIN ⸗

Next came another world tour, followed by a joint
show with Jay-Z, titled On the Run. For years the
couple had talked about a joint tour; each knew how
the other operated onstage and on the road. Now,
with two-year-old Blue Ivy along for the ride, the
timing was right to take the stage together. The
artists were on the run, but not quite like Bonnie
and Clyde, the criminal duo who had inspired
their first collaboration. "We're on the run from
everything. On the run from becoming a cliché. On
the run from doing the same thing again," Jay-Z
told reporters.

Beyoncé and Jay-Z kicked off a sold-out On the
Run tour on June 25, 2014, at Sun Life Stadium in
Miami, Florida, and ended it on September 13 at the
Stade de France in Paris. Fans poured into arenas
around the world to listen to the top songs by two of
the most powerful and influential artists of all time.
Images of the couple, their private wedding ceremony,
and their family flashed on a screen behind them as
they walked up and down two long runways dividing
the crowd.

⪤ LETTING LIFE IN ⪥

In 2016, Beyoncé released *Lemonade*, her sixth album and second visual project, which sold 485,000 copies in the first week. *Lemonade*, which is divided into eleven chapters, was the bestselling album of 2016 and was nominated for nine Grammys.

It seemed that Beyoncé was never going to slow down, constantly recording new material and relentlessly rehearsing for tours and shows. But in 2017, something happened that forced her to stop and take stock of everything. She had planned to perform at the annual Coachella Valley Music and Arts Festival in Indio, California, but she was surprised with news from her doctor that she was pregnant again. Beyoncé got another shock when she found out she was having twins!

Her body began to change, and she was unable to perform the energetic dance routines so integral to her performances. She delayed her Coachella appearance in order to rest during her pregnancy and spend time with Blue Ivy.

While she was pregnant, Beyoncé developed preeclampsia, a dangerous condition that causes high blood pressure in expectant mothers. Because one of the twins' heartbeats paused a few times, Beyoncé had to undergo an emergency cesarean section. On June 13, 2017, Beyoncé and Jay-Z welcomed their twins, Rumi and Sir.

I feel like I'm a new woman in a new chapter of my life. I'm not even trying to be who I was. It's so beautiful that children do that to you.

In 2018, her plan to perform at Coachella was back on track. Beyoncé would be the first black woman to headline the festival, and she was determined to pay homage to her African American heritage during the performance. Preparation for the set required four months of music rehearsals and four months of dance rehearsals.

"I studied my history. I studied my past. And I put every mistake, all of my triumphs, my twenty-two-year career into my two-hour Homecoming performance." —Beyoncé

Beyoncé wanted her Coachella performance to have the same atmosphere as the battle-of-the-bands competitions she'd attended back in high school. She called the events "the highlight of my year." She wanted her set to be something more than a fun show. "Instead of me pulling out my flower crown," she told the press, "it was important for me to bring our culture to Coachella. We were able to create a free, safe space where none of us were marginalized."

She had a demanding rehearsal schedule, along with a six-year-old and new twins in her trailer. Beyoncé cut out bread, dairy, sugar, carbs, meat, fish, and alcohol to meet her performance goals, and pushed her body to the limits of what was possible.

On the Coachella stage, she first wore blue-jean shorts, a glittery hoodie, and white tassel boots, before changing into an array of other dazzling costumes. The show included a huge marching band, along with a twirler and two break-dancers. Beyoncé's performance spanned her entire career, including her time with Destiny's Child. She once again welcomed Kelly and Michelle to the stage as the huge crowd went wild. One of the most unexpected moments of the performance was Beyoncé's rendition of "Lift Every Voice and Sing," sometimes referred to as the black national anthem. Her performance was one of the most watched Coachella videos on YouTube ever, and became known as "Beychella."

Act 1

1. INTRO

2. CRAZY IN LOVE

3. FREEDOM

4. LIFT EVERY VOICE AND S

5. FORMATION

6. SORRY / KITTY KAT

7. BOW DOWN

"Lift Every Voice and Sing"

In 1900, author and civil rights activist James Weldon Johnson wrote "Lift Every Voice and Sing," a poem celebrating black unity. At the turn of the twentieth century, though slavery had been abolished, Jim Crow laws were introduced across all former Confederate states, limiting black people's opportunities and forcing black and white people to live separate lives.

In "Lift Every Voice and Sing," Johnson encourages black people to "sing a song full of the faith that the dark past has taught us, sing a song full of the hope that the present has brought us." In 1920, "Lift Every Voice and Sing" became the official song of the National Association for the Advancement of Colored People and is often referred to as the black national anthem.

On April 17, 2019, Netflix released *Homecoming*, an in-depth look at Beyoncé's Coachella set, giving fans an insight into just how much performing means to this legendary singer. The documentary included quotes from influential black leaders and artists who have inspired Beyoncé and her work.

CONCLUSION

MUSIC ROYALTY

After more than twenty years at the top of
her game, Beyoncé continues to push creative
boundaries. Her family, friends, fellow artists, and
members of her fan club, the Beyhive, provide a
support network, but there's no doubt that Beyoncé
owes most of her success to nobody but herself.
Her drive, determination, and ceaseless striving for
perfection have ensured she will be remembered for
years, if not centuries, to come.

"In addition to being just
a beautiful young woman, she's been
a role model and a powerful presence
for young girls and women all around
the world. I'm very proud of her.
I'm very proud of the woman
she is." —Michelle Obama

THE BEYHIVE

Anyone with an interest in Beyoncé knows that her fans are some of the most dedicated and organized in the world. The Beyhive is a virtual community started by Beyoncé's management company. It's as busy as it sounds, ensuring that her millions of fans are the first to know about performances, merchandise, and music news. In her many award acceptance speeches, Beyoncé is quick to thank the fans who follow and love her.

In 2019, a picture that Beyoncé posted on her Instagram account, showing her facing Nala, the character she voices in the remake of Disney's *The Lion King*, reached almost 2.5 million likes in just one hour.

In addition to books, films, and, of course, music records, Beyoncé's merchandise spans everything from perfumes to sportswear. But even with so many different commercial ventures, Beyoncé tries to stay true to who she dreamed of being as a little girl.

"I don't really like to call myself a brand, and I don't like to think of myself as a brand. I'm a singer, a songwriter, a musician, and a performer. And an actress, and all the other things that I do. When you add it all together, some might call it a brand, but that's not my focus." —Beyoncé

It's vital to Beyoncé that decisions about the music, images, and information she releases are her own. In the momentous year of 2011, when she took the management of her career and her music into her own hands, she showed the determination and directness for which she is well known. She decided to build her "own empire and show other women when you get to this point in your career, you don't have to go sign with someone else and share your money and your success—you do it yourself."

For Beyoncé, it's important to show her fans that they, too, can make decisions about their own lives.

⋛ PRESENTING HER POLITICS ⋚

As Beyoncé's career has gone on, she has become more vocal about her political opinions. From backing Barack Obama's campaign to referencing the Black Lives Matter movement in her video for "Formation," Beyoncé is using her platform to raise awareness about issues affecting the United States and the world. Through her music and accompanying videos, she hopes to draw attention to the injustice she sees and to make a difference.

Stop Shooting US

Black Lives Matter

Black Lives Matter (BLM) is a movement against racism and violence toward black people. BLM holds protests against discrimination and racial inequality, as well as police killings of black people. The movement began on Twitter in 2013, when a white neighborhood watch captain was acquitted after shooting a black high school student, and the hashtag #BlackLivesMatter started trending.

Beyoncé paid tribute to the movement in her video for "Formation," where the phrase "Stop shooting us" is graffitied on a wall behind a young man facing off against a line of police officers.

Beyoncé's story teaches her fans one thing for sure. As much as they discuss and dream, it's impossible to predict what she will do next. Will she tour and collaborate with Jay-Z again? Will she step deeper into the world of politics? Could Queen Bey one day become president?

What is certain is that whatever she does will be her decision, and she will reveal her plans when she is ready.

$\overline{}$ ARTIST LOVE $\overline{}$

Within the music industry, fellow artists have been
quick to praise Beyoncé for her passion and hard work.
Over the years, the once painfully shy and quiet child
blossomed into a confident leader. She has evolved
into a global superstar who continues to inspire
through her music, business, and charitable work.

"I'm such a fan. . . .
Obviously, Queen Bey till
the day I die."
—Adele

"It's like normal for everyone
to love Beyoncé, but I love her
more than that amount, like more
than the normal amount. . . .
She's awesome."
—Taylor Swift

"I'm always, just like
always, in awe of her
talent. . . . I love working
with Bey. She's incredible.
Whenever she's ready to
work, I'm ready to work."
—Drake

"Just her name alone defines
greatness. . . . Here I am with
someone who I admire so much
just cause [she's] so driven. She
told me I killed it. That really
resonates with me."
—Nicki Minaj

Over the years, Beyoncé has performed for audiences around the world, but her contributions offstage are equally significant. She has supported more than thirty-seven charitable organizations and thirty-three causes, providing aid to those most in need of help.

The BeyGood Foundation supports organizations locally and globally. One of the foundation's projects works with St. John's United Methodist Church to build housing and community youth centers near her old Houston neighborhood.

"I've known Beyoncé since she was a little girl. She grew up at St. John's. . . . [She] has been an amazing friend and generous supporter."
—Pastor Rudy Rasmus, St. John's Church

One of Beyoncé's great strengths has always been her ability to work with others, valuing their unique contributions while having the confidence to speak up for her own views and vision. Over the years she has worked with many skilled producers and artists, launching successful albums and smaller projects.

Everything Beyoncé does is on her terms. Where some celebrities promote their work with endless magazine stories and interviews, Beyoncé has always kept the media at arm's length, allowing the public to see only what she wants people to see, when she's ready to let them see it. Perhaps the most exciting thing about this iconic superstar is her ability to surprise her fans again and again. Trends change, celebrities come and go, but Queen Bey is here to stay.

Timeline

Billboard unveils the Hot 100 chart.

December 4
Shawn Corey Carter (Jay-Z) i born in Brooklyn New York.

1958 1959 1969

May 4
Frank Sinatra is among the winners at the First Annual Grammy Awards.

Girls Tyme forms and begins performing together.

1988 1990

Beyoncé sings "Imagine" by John Lennon during her first talent show—and wins.

June 24
Solange Piaget Knowles is born in Houston, Texas.

1981   1986

September 4
Beyoncé Giselle Knowles is born in Houston, Texas.

Girls Tyme signs with Columbia Records and becomes Destiny's Child, with Mathew Knowles as the group's manager.

1992   1996   1998

Girls Tyme performs on the TV talent show *Star Search*.

February 17
Destiny's Child releases its first album, *Destiny's Child*.

LaTavia Roberson and LeToya Luckett leave Destiny's Child and are replaced by Michelle Williams and Farrah Franklin. Farrah leaves the band after five months.

Beyoncé appears in the TV film *Carmen: A Hip Hopera*.

2000   2001

September 11
Terrorists hijack four commercial airplanes and intentionally fly them into the Twin Towers at the World Trade Center in New York City and the Pentagon in Washington, DC. The fourth plane crashes into an empty field in Pennsylvania.

2006

Beyoncé appears in *Dreamgirls* and releases her album *B'Day*.

The *Oxford English Dictionary* adds the word *bootylicious* to its pages.

Destiny's Child
announces that the
group will disband
after its final tour.

2003   2005

June 23
Beyoncé releases
her debut solo
album, *Dangerously
in Love*.

January 20
Barack Obama
becomes president
of the United
States.

April 4
Beyoncé marries
Jay-Z.

2008   2009

November 12
Beyoncé releases
*I Am . . . Sasha
Fierce*, her third
solo album.

June 25
Michael Jackson
dies at his
home in Los
Angeles,
California.

June 24
Beyoncé releases
4, her fourth
studio album.

2010   2011   2012

January 31
Beyoncé wins
six Grammys in
one night.

January 7
Beyoncé and
Jay-Z welcome
a baby girl,
Blue Ivy.

June 13
Beyoncé and Jay-Z
welcome twins,
Rumi and Sir.

2017   2018

April 14
Beyoncé performs at
the annual Coachella
Valley Music and
Arts Festival in
Indio, California.

February 11
Whitney Houston dies at her home in Los Angeles, California.

2013

February 3
Beyoncé performs at the Super Bowl XLVII halftime show, along with former members of Destiny's Child.

Further Reading

→ *Beyoncé* (Ultimate Superstars) by Melanie Hamm (Studio Press, 2019)

→ *Beyoncé: Shine Your Light* by Sarah Warren and Geneva Bowers (HMH Books for Young Readers, 2019)

→ *Jay-Z* (Hip-Hop Headliners) by Roman P. Nacerous (Gareth Stevens Publishing, 2011)

→ *Music Legends* (40 Inspiring Icons) by Hervé Guilleminot (Wide Eyed Editions, 2018)

Websites

→ Beyonce.com
   Beyoncé's official website, with information
   about her music, upcoming tours, BeyGood
   Foundation, and merchandise.

→ billboard.com/charts
   Billboard's current top music charts.

Glossary

alter ego: A different version of oneself, or the opposite side of someone's personality.

choreography: The sequence of steps and movements in a dance performance.

collaborate: To work together with another person or organization to produce or create something.

congregation: An assembly of people, usually at a religious service.

contemporary: Relating to the present time.

depression: A serious medical condition that affects how you feel, think, and handle daily activities. Symptoms can include deep sadness, hopelessness, and loss of interest or pleasure in previously enjoyed activities, as well as changes in sleeping and eating.

Glossary

disband: To end or break up, as an organization or a group.

feminism: The belief that men and women should have equal rights and opportunities.

Jim Crow: Discriminatory laws and customs in the Southern United States between the 1860s and 1960s that restricted where black people could live, work, go to school, recreate, eat, drink, and even use the bathroom.

moonwalk: To perform a dance move in which the dancer slides backward while appearing to make forward walking motions.

preeclampsia: A serious condition that can occur in late pregnancy and result in high blood pressure in the mother.

Glossary

prodigy: A young person with exceptional talent or abilities.

protest: An organized demonstration meant to bring public attention to an injustice or a problem.

Index

Index

Index

Index

FOLLOW THE TRAIL!

TURN THE PAGE FOR A SNEAK PEEK AT THESE TRAILBLAZERS BIOGRAPHIES!

>>TRAIL BLAZERS

ALBERT EINSTEIN
THE GREATEST MIND IN PHYSICS

$E = mc^2$

Imagination is more important than knowledge.

PAUL VIRR

REBEL SCIENTIST

Albert passed his exams at Aarau with exceptional grades and, at the age of seventeen, became the youngest student to enter the Zurich Polytechnic. A rich aunt gave him an allowance to help him study, as Albert's parents were struggling financially.

It didn't take long before Albert's personality made its mark. Soon he was up to his old tricks, skipping lectures and annoying the professors with his attitude. Albert was disappointed that physics was only a small part of the program. He found some of the teaching out of date, especially when compared to the exciting ideas he was reading about in his spare time. Before long, Albert was spending most of his time studying the "masters of theoretical physics" at home. He borrowed lecture notes from his friend Marcel Grossmann to catch up, but Albert's absence was noticed by his teachers. It even led to the mathematics professor describing Albert as a "lazy dog."

But Albert was never lazy. Whenever he got the chance, he would talk about physics or philosophy. Around this time, Albert met Michele Besso at a musical evening. It was the start of a lifelong friendship. Conversations with Michele helped shape Albert's ideas.

Theoretical physics is a branch of science that uses math to try to explain the world around us and predict what might happen in the future. It creates models that help us visualize and understand the behavior of things in complex systems—like the universe!

Albert loved theoretical physics, but he also enjoyed practical experiments and working in the laboratory. However, his tendency to push things to the limit backfired one day, and he blew up one of his experiments!

What Is Light?

For centuries, scientists had argued about what light actually was. When you heat an iron poker, some of the heat energy is turned into light. As the poker gets hotter, it glows red, orange, and then white. German physicist Max Planck was interested in how energy, temperature, and the color of heated objects are related. He discovered that energy doesn't flow steadily but is transferred in specific packets, each of which is called a quantum (plural: quanta).

CHRISTIAAN HUYGENS   JAMES CLERK MAXWELL

Max couldn't figure out why. That was where Albert came in.

Albert explained how the specific colors produced by hot objects are due to light acting as a stream of particles. Each particle or quantum of light carries a specific packet of energy. The higher the frequency of the light, the bigger the packet of energy. Each frequency corresponds to a different color.

The Famous Equation

As if special relativity wasn't enough to make 1905 a year of scientific miracles, Albert finished by writing a short paper about energy and mass. In this almost casual postscript to special relativity, Albert noted how energy and mass are essentially the same—they can be converted into each other. This brief afterthought included the first version of the now-famous equation:

$$E = mc^2$$

E is energy, *m* is mass,
and *c* is the speed of light.

Albert's equation revealed how vast amounts of energy could be released from tiny amounts of matter. He had just described the source of the nuclear power that lights up the stars.

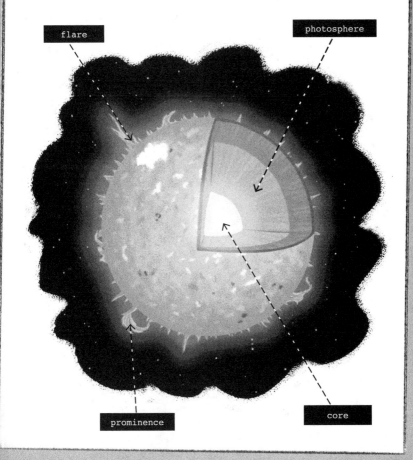

flare

photosphere

prominence

core

⋛ HARRIET'S ESCAPE ⋚

That night, Harriet went about her usual chores. John was hardly speaking to her these days, and they spent most evenings in silence. When she knew John was sound asleep, she got up quietly and helped herself to some ash cake (a type of bread), a piece of salt herring, and her wedding quilt.

Rather than set off into the woods, Harriet decided to head for Bucktown to the farm on the edge of the town. She was going to ask that white woman she had met by the road for assistance. It was a risky move—although the woman had said she'd help, Harriet couldn't know whether she'd really meant it, or how committed she would be to her offer once she discovered that Harriet was a runaway.

She uttered a quick prayer, walked toward the woman's door, and gently tapped on it. In the stillness of the night, the knock sounded so loud. The door opened, and the Quaker woman appeared. To Harriet's great relief, the woman nodded and asked Harriet to come in. She led Harriet into the kitchen and told her to sit down. She wrote two names on a piece of paper, then gave Harriet directions of where to go next.

The first stop, or station, on the Underground
Railroad was another farm; Harriet couldn't miss it—
there were two white posts with round knobs on them.
The people there would give her food and clothing and
keep her safe until it was time to move to the next place.

FAME AND FORTUNE

As she grew more famous, it became difficult for Harriet to make as many trips down South as before. Still desperate to help the Underground Railroad's efforts, in 1858 she began lecturing at locations all over the North. Her firsthand accounts of the Underground Railroad and its workings proved very popular, and she raised even more money to help fugitives, station masters, and conductors fighting to free slaves.

She was invited to speak in the parlor rooms of high society in Concord and Boston. In these anti-slavery speeches, Harriet told fascinating stories of her narrow escapes. Money poured in as more and more people heard about her amazing rescues.

HARRIET'S STORIES

One time, Harriet was traveling during the day in her home state of Maryland. She was wearing a large sunbonnet and kept her head bowed, but when she passed a former employer, Harriet worried that she would be recognized. Luckily, she'd just bought a couple of chickens at the market.

Thinking quickly, she opened the cage of chickens, which fluttered and squawked, causing an awful noise and diverting attention from herself.

On a different occasion, Harriet was traveling in a railroad car and noticed two gentlemen quietly discussing whether she was the woman on the Wanted poster at the station. Never one to panic, she simply picked up a newspaper and began to "read" it. Harriet Tubman was known to be illiterate—so this woman reading the paper studiously surely could not be the fugitive!

BEASTS AT THE BIRCHES

Despite the war, Jane spent many happy years at the Birches. To her delight, the house had a large, rambling garden, where she played for hours on end. Jane's favorite tree was a big beech tree. She loved it so much that Danny gave it to her, officially, for her tenth birthday. Jane was often found perched on a branch of her tree, reading a book or doing her homework.

Jane also collected a large number of pets, including a tortoise called Johnny Walker, a slow worm called Solomon, a canary called Peter, not to mention several terrapins, guinea pigs, and cats. Jane and Judy also had their own "racing" snails with numbers painted on their shells. The girls kept the snails in a wooden box covered with a piece of glass and with no bottom, so that the snails could feed on fresh dandelion leaves as the girls moved the box around the lawn.

Animal Fact File

Name: Peter

Animal: Canary

Behavior: Slept in a cage
           but was free to
           fly around during the day.

⋛ THE ALLIGATOR CLUB ⋚

As well as watching the birds, squirrels, foxes, insects, and spiders that came into the garden, Jane started her own nature club. It was called the Alligator Club and had four members—Jane; Judy; and their two best friends, Sally and Sue Cary, who came to stay at the Birches during the summer breaks. Each girl had to choose

an animal as her code name— Jane was Red Admiral, Sally was Puffin, Sue was Ladybird, and Judy was Trout.

Primate, Monkey, or Ape?

There are more than three hundred species of primates. They all share many features, including large brains compared to the size of their bodies, forward-facing eyes, and flexible limbs and hands for grasping. But, while monkeys and apes (chimps, bonobos, gorillas, orangutans, and gibbons) are both primates, monkeys are not the same as apes. Here's how to tell them apart:

APES

Larger brains

Shoulders designed for swinging from branch to branch

Larger bodies and broader chests

No tails

MONKEYS

Smaller brains

Bodies built for running across branches, not swinging

Smaller bodies and narrower chests

Most have tails

Over the next few months, Jane's frustration grew. Sometimes, she didn't see any chimps for days, and when she did, she couldn't get close enough to observe them properly. So as not to startle the chimps, Jane wore clothes that blended in with the forest, and sat patiently for hours. The minute she tried to move nearer, the chimps scampered off. She was getting worried that if she didn't get results soon, Louis would have to cancel the project, and she would have to leave Gombe.

Sweater

Food and drink

BEANS BEANS

Notebook and pens

Binoculars

Sleeping bag

Bagged lunch

COMING SOON . . .

>>TRAIL BLAZERS

Simone Biles

Stephen Hawking

Martin Luther King Jr.

J. K. Rowling